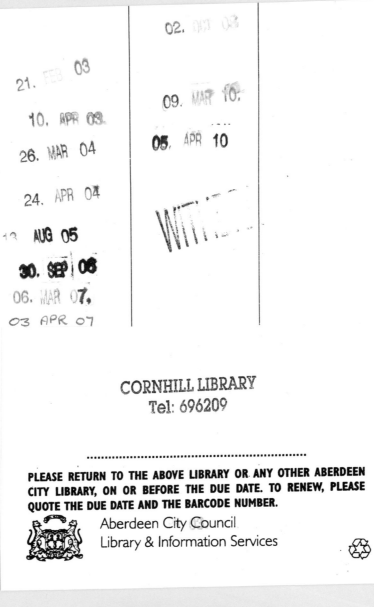

Living in
France

Ruth Thomson

Photography by David Hampton

FRANKLIN WATTS
LONDON • SYDNEY

First published in 2002 by
Franklin Watts,
96 Leonard Street,
London EC2A 4XD

Franklin Watts Australia,
56 O'Riordan Street,
Alexandria, NSW 2015

Copyright © Franklin Watts 2002

Series editor: Ruth Thomson
Series designer: Edward Kinsey
Photographs by David Hampton except
page 9 Wimenet, Parc du Futuroscope

With thanks to Virginia Chandler

914.4

A CIP catalogue record for this book is available from the British
Library

Dewey Classification 914.4

ISBN 0 7496 4639 X

Printed and bound in Malaysia

Contents

This is France

France is the second biggest country in Europe. The French call it 'the Hexagon' because of its six-sided shape. It has borders with six other countries.

The island of Corsica in the Mediterranean and the distant lands of Guiana in South America, Guadeloupe and Martinique in the Caribbean, and Réunion in the Indian Ocean are part of the French nation too.

△ **Dense forests**
Forests cover a quarter of the country. They give timber for industry, shelter for wildlife and are popular with walkers.

△ **The coastline**
The sea borders three sides of France. The Atlantic coast of Brittany is wild and rugged. Its rocky inlets shelter busy fishing ports.

◁ **Lush pastures**
France has an ideal climate for farming. In the west, farms have orchards and small hedged fields where dairy cattle graze.

4

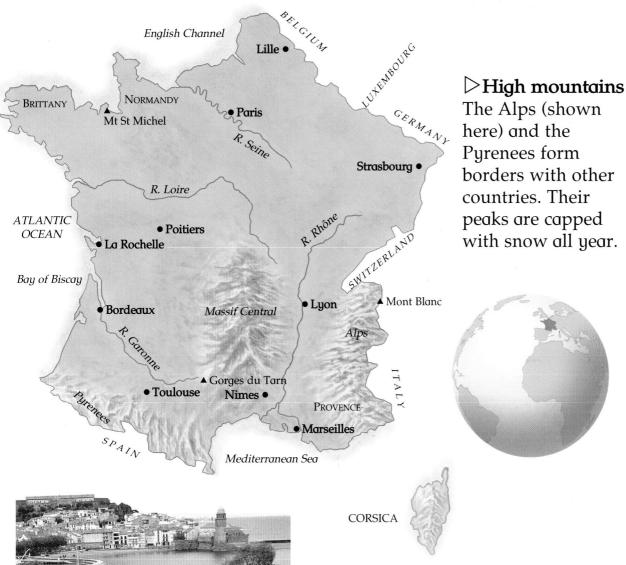

English Channel

BELGIUM

Lille •

LUXEMBOURG

NORMANDY

▲ Mt St Michel

• Paris

GERMANY

R. Seine

BRITTANY

Strasbourg •

R. Loire

ATLANTIC
OCEAN

• Poitiers

• La Rochelle

R. Rhône

SWITZERLAND

Bay of Biscay

• Bordeaux

Massif Central

• Lyon

▲ Mont Blanc

R. Garonne

Alps

ITALY

▲ Gorges du Tarn

• Toulouse   Nimes •

PROVENCE

Pyrenees

• Marseilles

SPAIN

Mediterranean Sea

CORSICA

▷ High mountains

The Alps (shown here) and the Pyrenees form borders with other countries. Their peaks are capped with snow all year.

◁ The sunny south

The hot, sunny Mediterranean coast is crowded in summer with millions of holidaymakers. Olive and fruit trees, fields of lavender and herbs grow inland.

Fact Box

Capital: Paris
Population: 58.6 million
Official language: French
Main religion: Roman Catholic
Highest mountain: Mont Blanc (4,807 m)
Longest river: Loire (1,012 km)
Biggest cities: Marseilles, Lyon, Lille, Toulouse, Bordeaux
Currency: Euro

Paris – the capital

Paris is by far the biggest and most important city in France. One in five French people live in the capital and its surrounding area. It is the centre of French government and of banking and business, culture and fashion. It is also the hub of the country's road and railway network.

△ **The Champs Elysées**
Military parades and the last stage of the Tour de France bicycle race take place on this wide avenue, full of smart shops.

◁ **The Eiffel Tower**
Over 320 metres high, this iron tower was built in 1889 for the Universal Exhibition. It took two years to build, using more than two million rivets!

▽ **La Défense**
Thousands of people work in a huge office building shaped like an arch at La Défense, one of the business centres of Paris.

△ **Notre Dame**
This Gothic cathedral stands on an island, the Ile de la Cité, in the middle of the River Seine.

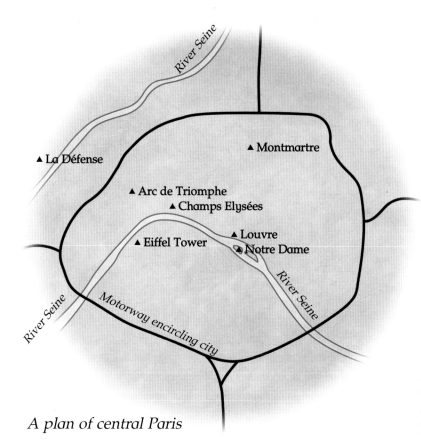

A plan of central Paris

The world capital of tourism

The museums and monuments of Paris are famous the world over. Eleven million foreign tourists flock to Paris each year to see its sights, to eat in its famous restaurants and to shop in its luxury stores.

△ **The River Seine**
The River Seine runs through Paris, crossed by 37 bridges. Visitors can take a ride along the river on a boat called a *bâteau mouche*.

▷ **The Louvre**
Once the palace of French kings, the Louvre is the world's biggest art museum. The entrance is under a modern glass pyramid.

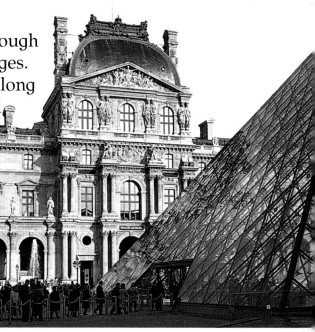

7

Famous sights

France is full of treasures from its long and rich history. Cave paintings of animals and hunters date back to prehistoric times. Traces of the Roman conquest, when the country was called Gaul, can be seen in ruined villas, amphitheatres and bridges.

Every period has left its mark – from the cathedrals, towns and castles of the Middle Ages and the castles (*châteaux*) of Renaissance nobles, to the most up-to-date buildings of today.

△ **The Maison Carrée, Nîmes**
The Romans built a city, with temples, theatres and baths, at Nîmes, in the south of France. This Roman temple honoured the grandsons of the emperor Augustus.

▷ **Mont Saint Michel**
This monastery was built on top of a granite island off the Normandy coast, in the Middle Ages. Now it has a million visitors a year.

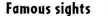

△ The Tarn Gorge

France is also famous for its natural wonders. The rushing river Tarn in southern France has cut spectacular gorges through the rocks.

A selection of tourist guides and brochures

△ The Château of Chambord

Chambord is the largest of the châteaux in the Loire valley. King François I transformed the medieval castle into a splendid Renaissance palace with 440 rooms and 83 staircases.

△ Futuroscope

The Futuroscope theme park, near Poitiers, houses the latest audio-visual shows. Its futuristic buildings include cinemas with circular or 3-D screens.

Living in towns and cities

More than three-quarters of French people live in cities or towns. Many town centres are full of historic buildings, which have often been cleaned and restored.

The heart of a city is usually a large square (*place*) where the town hall stands. Above its door flies the French flag, the *Tricolore* (three colours). The *place* may have restaurants and cafés, with a church and market nearby.

△**Riverside towns**
Most towns are situated on or near one of France's many rivers. Sometimes, violent rains can cause damaging floods.

◁**The mayor**
Every city, town, and village elects a council, with a mayor as its leader. The mayor wears the *Tricolore* sash of office for ceremonies.

△**Car-free streets**
Cars are banned from many city centre streets and squares. These are pleasant, safe places to stroll and shop.

◁ **Town church**
All towns have a large church or cathedral near the centre. The main religion in France is Roman Catholicism. However, fewer people go to church regularly now than in the past.

▽ **Town signs**
On the road into every town or village is a sign with its name. On the way out of town is the same sign with a line through it. This sign shows the road number as well.

△ **Living in flats**
Many people live on the outskirts of large towns, in flats on high-rise estates.

Most areas have local tourist brochures

Around town

Cafés are a central part of town life. They open from early morning till late at night for coffee, drinks and food. People of all ages come to meet their friends, read the newspapers provided, play cards or the pinball machine (*le flipper*), or watch a football match on the bar TV.

△**City faces**
Over the years, people of many countries and races have come to live and work in France. Many have French nationality.

◁**Children's menu**
Some restaurants serve cheap three-course meals for children.

▷**Street cafés**
People enjoy sitting outside at cafés to watch the world go by. The tables are shaded by awnings.

▽ A Morris column

This pillar-shaped billboard advertises the latest films, concerts or plays.

Evenings in town

Town centres are often lively in the evening. The cafés fill up again, as people leave work and meet for a drink before going to a restaurant, the cinema or theatre.

◁ Parks

Town parks are very well looked after. They have gravel paths and formal flower beds.

◁ Opening times

In smaller towns, shops shut for two hours or more at lunchtime.
But they stay open in the evening.

△ Street signs

French streets – and schools and public buildings – are often named after a saint or a famous person. Voltaire was a French writer of the 18th century.

13

Living in the country

Farming has always been important to France. Farmland covers more than half the country. It produces enough food both to feed its people and to sell abroad.

Sixty years ago, half the population lived in the country. Today, it's only a quarter. In rich farming areas, modern machines and methods can produce more food than before, with fewer workers.

▷ **Vineyards**
Wine is one of France's most valuable products. Vineyards are found in most regions. Growers prune the vines by hand.

◁ **A country treasure**
In the autumn, country people hunt for prized wild mushrooms. They may sell these at the local village market.

△ **The village square**
Most villages have a square with a church and a memorial to local men killed in the two World Wars.

△**Modern farming**
On the fertile plains, farmers use enormous, expensive machines to spray and harvest crops in vast, open fields.

▽**Country homes**
Once, country farms and houses were built in the local style, using the stone, brick or wood of the region. New homes tend to look all alike and are built of the same modern materials.

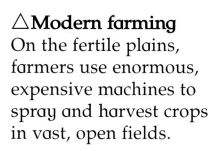

Empty villages

Young people are leaving the country to find work in towns. As villages in remote areas empty, their shops and schools close. Villages near big cities are thriving, as city commuters move into new houses built on farmland.

◁**Travelling shop**
As village shops close down, country people depend on visits from the travelling grocer, butcher and baker in their vans.

Shopping

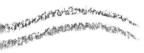

Busy modern life means people find it easier to shop in out-of-town hypermarkets. These giant stores sell everything under one roof – food, furniture, computers and TVs and do-it-yourself supplies. They open for long hours and are cheap.

The French appreciate fresh, quality food and still use specialist shops. They enjoy going to the local market, which is a social event as well as a chance to buy local produce.

Butcher (*Boucherie*)

Fishmonger (*Poissonerie*)

Supermarket sign

△**Pastry shop (*pâtisserie*)**
Pâtisseries sell fruit tarts, éclairs, meringues and other pastries. Fancy cakes can be made to order for a special occasion.

▷**French bread**
The baker (*boulangerie*) is open every day of the year! The traditional *baguette* (seen here) goes stale quickly, so people buy it fresh once, or often twice, each day.

▷**Local shops**
Specialist food shops offer high quality produce. Supermarkets often sell clothes and items for the home as well as food.

◁ **A retail park**
Superstores are grouped round a
vast car park on the outskirts of
cities. It is hard for small shops
in town to compete with them.

▷ **Tobacconist (*tabac*)**
Places that sell tobacco
always have an orange
'carrot' sign on the
outside. They sell
lottery tickets, phone
cards and stamps,
cards and sweets –
as well as cigarettes.

◁ **The market**
Every town has a
market at least once
a week, selling fruit,
vegetables and cheese.
Some stallholders sell
local produce, such as
eggs or herbs, grown
in their own
allotments.

The tabac *sells a
wide range of items.*

On the move

The French are keen motorists. Eight out of ten families own a car. They mostly buy French models – Renault, Peugeot or Citroën. People prefer to drive to work, and to use their cars for weekend outings and holidays.

More than 6,000km of motorways link towns in France. These have frequent parking spots (*aires*) where motorists can rest and eat.

△Cycling

In towns, bicycle lanes are often separated from other road traffic, to make cycling safe.

▷A moped (*mobylette*)

Mopeds and scooters are popular with young people. They can ride these from the age of 14, after passing a test.

Toll receipt

Motorway sign

▷Motorway tolls

Drivers take a ticket just before they join a motorway (*autoroute*). When they leave it, they pay a toll, according to the distance they have travelled.

18

◁ The Normandy Bridge

This great bridge, over 2km long, spans the river Seine in Normandy. It links northern and western France.

△ Michelin man

Bibendum is the mascot of Michelin tyres. He appears on Michelin maps, guides and adverts.

◁ High speed trains

The TGV travels at 200km an hour. It takes 3 hours to travel from Paris to Marseilles – 757km.

◁ Punching tickets

Passengers must punch their tickets in a machine before boarding their train.

▽ The métro

However long the journey on a *métro*, the ticket always costs the same. People can save money by buying ten tickets at a time.

Trains

The railway system is very efficient. High speed trains, known as TGV (*Train à Grande Vitesse*), zoom between cities. Slower trains go to the suburbs and between towns. Big cities, such as Paris, Lyon and Marseilles, have an underground railway, called the *métro*.

19

Family life

The French think family life is important. Different generations may live further away from one another than in the past, but they often get together for holidays and reunions. In the school holidays, grandparents may look after children of working parents.

Most homes have all the latest equipment. Nearly all of them have a TV, and half own two. There are five channels, plus pay TV, cable and satellite.

△ **Family pets**
France holds the European record for the number of pets. One in three families has a dog, one in five a cat.

△ **Evening meals**
Three out of four French women go out to work. But most families still eat together in the evening, at around 8pm.

◁ **Sunday lunch**
Weekends often mean a big family meal at grandma's home in the country, or at a restaurant.

▷ **Weekend outings**
Weekends are a chance to enjoy sport together – hiking, cycling or going to a football, rugby or basketball match.

△ Games
Video and computer games are popular and so are comic books.

△ Happy birthday! (*Joyeux Anniversaire!*)
The French celebrate birthdays with a cake and cards. They often sing the happy birthday song in English!

Asterix and Lucky Luke are among the favourite comic book characters for both children and adults.

Time to eat

France is well-known for its fine cooking and its good restaurants. The French always mark a special occasion with a grand meal, with five courses or more.

France produces a huge variety of foods. Every region is known for its own particular local produce or dish.

△**Seafood**
Platters of freshly caught oysters, mussels, crab and other shell-fish are served in restaurants by the sea.

△**Foreign flavours**
Immigrants have brought their own specialities. In big cities, there may be Algerian, Tunisian, Vietnamese and Chinese food shops and restaurants.

Cassoulet from south-west France – a dish of beans, sausage and duck

Dijon mustard

Olives from the south of France

Three of the 400 French cheeses

Mineral water from Evian

Lentils from central France

Oil and herbs from Provence

Boar pâté from central France

Sweet pancake from Brittany

Sardines from Brittany

Dried sausage from the Auvergne

▷ Breakfast

A typical breakfast is cereal or a slice of crusty bread and jam, fruit juice, yoghurt and a bowl of hot chocolate.

◁ All sorts of bread

As well as bread, bakers sell sweet breads, buttery croissants, chocolate-filled croissants and raisin buns, which people often buy for breakfast.

△ Eating out

In summer, squares and pavements are crowded with restaurant tables. People may spend several hours enjoying their meal.

◁ Fast food

Many traditional restaurants have given way to fast-food outlets. These sell burgers, sandwiches, pancakes and pizzas.

23

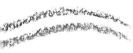

School time

In France, children must go to school from 6 to 16 years old. Most start at the age of three, in a state nursery school, and stay at school until they are 18. French children have the longest school day in Europe.

Primary school is from 9am till 5pm (with a two-hour break for three-course lunch, often in the canteen). There is homework to do after school. Much of the day is spent on reading, spelling, grammar and maths – and there is no religious education.

◁ **Free time**
There is no school on Wednesday afternoons. That is the time for playing sport in local clubs, or other activities, such as music or dance.

△ **One-class school**
Unlike most schools, this country school has only one class and one teacher. Children of varying ages are grouped together. For secondary school, they will journey by bus to the nearest town.

▷**School equipment**
Children have to buy their own exercise books, pens and ruler. The white board is for quick spelling tests in class.

△**Saturday school**
In some towns, there is school on Saturday mornings instead of Wednesday mornings.

▷**School books**
Pupils keep their books at home, and take what they need to school each day. Their school bags can be very heavy – some even have wheels!

Drawing book

Class workbook

Music exercise book

Handwriting book

Grammar exercise book

Pupil's school report

25

Having fun

With five weeks of holiday a year and shorter working hours than in the past, the French have plenty of leisure time. Seven out of ten people play sport. They prefer individual ones such as tennis, skiing or judo.

The major team sport is football – young players dream of joining the *Bleus*, the French national team, winners of the World Cup in 1998 and European champions in 2000.

△ **Pétanque**
The aim of this popular game is to bowl a heavy metal ball as close as possible to a small wooden one.

△ **Roller-blading**
Some towns organise car-free Sundays, when skaters, cyclists and walkers can take over the streets for the day.

◁ **Table football**
Coin-operated table football games (*baby-foot*), are often found in cafés and youth clubs.

◁**Family picnic**
On fine weekends, people from towns and cities often spend the day in the countryside.

△**Multiplex cinema**
Out-of-town multi-screen cinemas show up to 15 different films at a time.

Going on outings

Many French enjoy fishing, hunting or having large family picnics. They are also great cinema-goers. Increasingly, they have videos for watching films at home.

▷**Video kiosk**
People can rent a video, using a credit card, at any time of day or night at one of these automatic kiosks.

Holidays and celebrations

At the beginning of July and August, roads and railway stations are packed as the French set off on holiday. The great majority of them stay in France.

Half go to the seaside, but nearly as many go to the countryside or mountains for activity holidays – hiking, kayaking or climbing. Many save a week of their holidays for winter sports in the Alps or Pyrenees.

▽ Sightseeing
The French are proud of their heritage. They like to explore historical sites and monuments on holiday.

△ Going to the seaside
Visitors crowd the beaches in summer. Some resorts organise beach clubs with games and activities for children.

◁ Holiday activities
Camping, water skiing, walking and fishing are all popular holiday activities.

◁**Food festivals**
Many regions hold fairs to celebrate their local produce. At this apple fair, people can sample many different varieties, as well as buy tarts and jams, juice and cider.

△**A pardon**
In Brittany, saints' days are marked with a pardon, when villagers parade in their traditional costumes with music and dancing.

▷**Bastille day, 14th July**
This national holiday celebrates the attack on the Bastille prison at the start of the French Revolution in 1789. A funfair comes to town, people dance and there are fireworks.

Fairs and festivals

Throughout France, festivities mark special occasions. Some are linked to religion, like the Carnival parades before Lent. Others celebrate country traditions or a particular season of the year. Some are related to local or national historical events.

29

Going further

Look for French food

Have a good look in a supermarket and see how many foods you can find that have come from France.

What sorts of foods are they? Do the labels tell you which part of France they come from? Find the places on a map of France. What types of food come from each region?

Find a French pen pal

Ask your relatives, teachers, friends and neighbours if they know anyone of your age who lives in France and who might like to write to you. Tell your pen pal about your home, your interests and your friends.

Trade some postcards, stamps and stickers. Keep a scrapbook of things your pen pal sends you.

Make a tourist leaflet

Make a tourist leaflet about Paris or a French sight that interests you.

Fold a piece of paper into three overlapping flaps. Glue down some pictures cut out from magazines, newspapers or holiday brochures. Write short captions about them.

A useful place to get brochures and information about sights and places is:
The French Government Tourist Office,
178 Piccadilly,
London W1V 0AL

Websites

www.yahooligans.com/
Around_the_world/countries/France

www.sitesatlas.com/Europe/France

www.zipzapfrance.com

Glossary

Audio-visual The technology of sound and images used in cinema and TV.

Commuter A worker, living in the country or the town suburbs, who travels every day to work in a city business or office.

Currency The money used in a country.

French Revolution The great change that took place in France after 1789, when the people of France took over power from the King and the Church. They demanded freedom, justice and equality for all.

Gorge A deep, narrow opening cut into hills by a river.

Gothic A style of building in the 13th and 14th centuries. Churches were tall, with high pointed arches and windows.

Heritage The culture passed down through a country's history.

Hypermarket A huge self-service shop, bigger than a supermarket, that sell a wide range of goods.

Immigrants People who have left their country to come and live in another country.

Monastery A place where men belonging to a religious order, known as monks, live together.

Nationality Belonging to a particular country.

Population The number of people living in a country.

Prehistoric times The period between the first appearance of people (6 million years ago) and the invention of writing (about 3,500 years ago).

Renaissance Means rebirth in French. It is the name given to the time in the 15th and 16th century, in Europe, when new, exciting changes and discoveries happened in art and science.

Suburb An area outside a town centre where people live.

3-D screens Screens that give a feeling of depth (three dimensions), rather than just a flat image.

Vineyards Fields planted with grape vines.

Index

Page numbers in *italics* refer to entries in the fact box, on the map or in the glossary.